INSANELY ANNOYING JOKE BOOK

EGMONT
We bring stories to life

First published in Great Britain 2014
by Egmont UK Limited
The Yellow Building, 1 Nicholas Road,
London W11 4AN

Stay safe online. Any website addresses listed
in this book are correct at the time of going
to print. However, Egmont is not responsible
for content hosted by third parties. Please be
aware that online content can be subject to
change and websites can contain content that
is unsuitable for children. We advise that all
children are supervised when using the internet.

ISBN 978 1 4052 7134 9
57422/1
Printed in Great Britain

I'M AN ORANGE!

THEY SAY 'YOU ARE WHAT YOU EAT'. THAT'S WEIRD – I DON'T REMEMBER EATING A HILARIOUS COMEDIAN THIS MORNING!

WHAT DO YOU CALL AN ORANGE THAT PLAYS THE TRUMPET?
A TOOTY FRUITY! HAHAHAHA!

WHY DID THE ORANGE STOP ROLLING DOWN THE HILL?
'COZ HE RAN OUT OF JUICE!

WHAT DO YOU CALL A REVOLVING ORANGE?
A MERRY-GO-RIND.

WHAT'S ORANGE AND SOUNDS LIKE A PARROT?
A CARROT!

Hey, Pear! Hey, Pear! Pear! Ask me how you make an orange laugh!

Sigh How do you make an orange laugh?

Tickle its navel! Hahahahaha!

Groan

FRUITY FRIENDS

There's nothing I love more than making jokes about my fruity friends! And they love it, too!

WHAT'S KING KONG'S FAVOURITE FRUIT?
THE APE-RICOT!
GET IT? HAHAHAHAHA!

HEY, DO YOU KNOW WHICH APPLE HAS THE SHORTEST TEMPER?
IT'S A CRAB APPLE!

WHAT DID THE APPLE SKIN SAY TO THE APPLE?
I'VE GOT YOU COVERED!

WHEN IS AN APPLE NOT AN APPLE?
WHEN IT'S A PINEAPPLE!
HAHAHAHA!

HEY, BANANA! IF YOU WERE MADE INTO A PAIR OF SHOES, ***YOU'D BE SLIPPERS!*** GET IT? ***SLIPPERS?*** HAHAHAHA!

HOW DO YOU TEASE A BANANA?
BANANANANANANANANANANANANANANANA!

HEY, BANANA! DO YOU KNOW WHAT KIND OF KEY I'D NEED TO OPEN YOU?
A MONKEY!

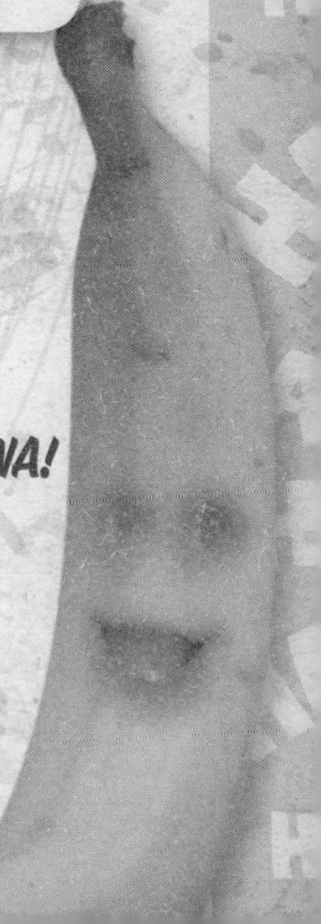

FRUITY FRIENDS FUNNIES

HEY, APPLE!

Why were the apple and orange alone?
BECAUSE THE BANANA SPLIT!

WHAT'S THE EASIEST WAY TO MAKE A BANANA SPLIT?
CUT IT IN HALF!

HEY, HEY COCONUT!
WHAT'S CRACKIN'?

HEY, COCONUT! WHEN YOU WERE CRACKED OPEN, DID YOU FEEL ***EMPTY INSIDE?***

HAHAHAHAHA!

Hey, Grape! Why don't you snore? Is it because you don't want to wake up the rest of the BUNCH?

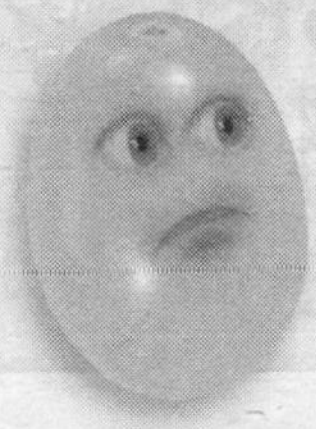

Why did Mrs. Grape leave Mr. Grape?
SHE WAS TIRED OF RAISIN KIDS!

HAHAHAHAHAHA!

What do you get when two strawberries meet?
A STRAWBERRY SHAKE!

AND WHAT DO YOU GET WHEN TWO STRAWBERRIES GO ON A DATE?
A STRAWBERRY CRUSH!

HEY, STRAWBERRY!

WHY ARE YOU CRYING? ***ARE YOU IN A JAM?***

HA HA HA HA HA!

VEG OUT!

Hey, Vegetables! Bet you wish you were as awesome as me and my fruity friends! Yeah!

WHAT KIND OF VEGETABLE IS JEALOUS?
THE GREEN BEAN!

GET IT? GET IT?

HEY, HEY SWEDE! IF YOU DIE, I RECKON THERE'LL BE A HUGE ***TURNIP*** AT YOUR FUNERAL. HAHAHAHA!

WHAT'S A TAXI DRIVER'S
FAVOURITE VEGETABLE?
A CAB-BAGE!
HAHAHAHA!

WHAT ARE TWO ROWS OF
CABBAGES CALLED?
A DUAL CABBAGEWAY!

HEY, CORN! DID YOU GET MAD
AT THE FARMER WHEN HE KEPT
PULLING YOUR *EARS?* HAHAHAHA!

HEY, RADISH! WHY ARE YOU SO SMART? I GUESS IT'S
BECAUSE YOU'RE SO *WELL RED!*

WHAT DO YOU CALL A RETIRED VEGETABLE?
A HAS-BEAN!
GET IT?

HAHA HA HA HA!

What do you call an angry pea?
GRUM-PEA!

VEG OUT AGAIN!

WHAT'S SMALL, RED AND WHISPERS? *A HOARSE RADISH.* HAHAHAHA!

HEY! DID YOU KNOW THAT POTATOES MAKE GREAT DETECTIVES? *YEAH, BECAUSE THEY ALWAYS HAVE THEIR EYES PEELED!* HAHAHAHA!

DO YOU KNOW WHAT YOU GET IF YOU EAT ONIONS AND BAKED BEANS? *TEAR GAS!* HAHAHAHA!

Hey, Baked Beans! Your can is a work of FART! I don't know how anyone could TRUMP that! Hahahaha!

What veggie can you find in a toilet?
A LEEK!
Get it?
ISN'T IT WEIRD HOW MUSHROOMS ALWAYS GROW CLOSE TOGETHER? I GUESS IT'S BECAUSE THEY DON'T NEED MUSHROOM. HAHAHAHA!
HEY, CABBAGE! KNOW WHY YOU'RE SO SMART? 'COZ YOU'VE GOT A BIG HEAD! HAHAHAHAHA!
What's the difference between broccoli and bogies?
KIDS DON'T EAT BROCCOLI ...

ATTACK OF THE ZOMBIE VEGETABLES!

Sigh
It all started when kids refused to eat their veggies and just threw them away. Now kitchens all over the world are overrun with zombie vegetables! And what do zombie vegetables eat, you ask? YEAH – FRUIT!

WHAT DO ZOMBIES EAT IN RESTAURANTS?
THE WAITER!

HEY, ZOMBIE PEPPER! WHEN YOU WERE TURNED INTO A ZOMBIE, WHAT DID YOU SHOUT?

GRAAAAAAINS!

HEY! HEY, ZOMBIE ONION! WHEN YOU MEET A NEW FRUIT, DO YOU SAY 'PLEASED TO EAT YOU'?
HEY, ZOMBIE CARROT! WHAT DO YOU LIKE TO EAT FOR DESSERT – ICE SCREAM?
Hey, Zombie Vegetables! You look DEAD TIRED! HAHAHAHAHA!

SILLY SALAD

My salad friends didn't want me to make jokes about them, but I just couldn't **LEAF** it alone! Hahahaha!

HEY, LETTUCE! YOU SHOULD QUIT WHILE YOU'RE *A-HEAD!* HAHAHAHA!

HEY, WHAT'S THE COLDEST SALAD INGREDIENT? *THE ICEBERG LETTUCE!*

Hey, what did the pickle say to the cucumber? I'M KIND OF A BIG DILL!

And why did the pickle stay home from school? BECAUSE HE FELT DILL! Hahahaha!

HEY YOU!
Hey, Carrot Batons! I'm really glad you guys could STICK AROUND! Hahahaha!
HEY, CELERY! LETTUCE ASKED ME TO PASS ON A MESSAGE. HE SAYS, 'QUIT STALKING ME!'

KNOCK KNOCK!

Is someone at the door? Is it a food delivery? New friends? **Yay! Hahahaha!**

KNOCK KNOCK!
WHO'S THERE?
BEAN!
BEAN WHO?
BEAN A WHILE SINCE I LAST SAW YOU!

KNOCK KNOCK!
WHO'S THERE?
FIGS!
FIGS WHO?
FIGS THE DOORBELL, IT'S BROKEN!

KNOCK KNOCK!
WHO'S THERE?
BANANA.
BANANA WHO?
BANANA SPLIT SO ICE CREAMED!

Knock knock!
Who's there?
Muffin.
Muffin who?
Muffin the matter with me, what about you?

HA HA HA HA HA HA
KNOCK KNOCK! WHO'S THERE? CASH! CASH WHO? NO THANKS, BUT I'D LIKE SOME PEANUTS!
Knock knock! Who's there? Four eggs. Four eggs who? FOUR EGGS AMPLE!
KNOCK KNOCK! WHO'S THERE? KETCHUP. KETCHUP WHO? KETCHUP TO ME AND I'LL TELL YOU!
Knock knock! Who's there? Pizza. Pizza who? PIZZA DA PIE!

Dry Humour

Man, it's dusty in this cupboard!

WHAT KIND OF BREAKFAST CEREAL IS THE COLDEST?
FROSTED FLAKES! HAHAHAHA!

HOW LONG SHOULD YOU COOK SPAGHETTI FOR?
ABOUT THIRTY CENTIMETRES!

MAN, THAT MUESLI CAN BE REALLY DANGEROUS. IF YOU'RE NOT CAREFUL, YOU CAN BE PULLED IN BY A *STRONG CURRANT!*

Hey, Multigrain Hoops!
Shouldn't you be called
DONUT SEEDS?
Hahahahaha!

HEY! WHAT DID THE TOASTER SAY TO THE LOAF? **'POP UP AND SEE ME SOMETIME!'** HAHAHAHA!

AND WHAT KIND OF CLOTHES DOES TOAST LIKE TO WEAR? **JAMMIES!**

OOH, A BAG OF NUTS! HEY, HEY BAG FACE! HEY BAG FACE! BAG FACE! IT LOOKS LIKE YOU HAD A LITTLE **PLASTIC SURGERY!** HAHAHAHAHA!

HEY, PRETZEL! WHAT'S YOUR FAVOURITE DANCE? **IS IT THE TWIST!** HAHAHAHAHA!

HEY! HEY! HEY!

WHAT DO YOU GET IF YOU CROSS A BISCUIT WITH A TUXEDO? **ONE SMART COOKIE!**

In the Fridge's Custardy

These fridge jokes are totally cool!

WHAT'S WHITE AND STANDS IN THE CORNER?
A NAUGHTY FRIDGE!

HEY, DO YOU KNOW WHY A FRIDGE IS THE BEST PRESENT? BECAUSE WHEN YOU GIVE IT TO SOMEONE YOU CAN WATCH THEIR FACE *LIGHT UP* AS THEY OPEN IT! HAHAHAHA!

HEY, WHICH VITAMIN TASTES OF SALT?
IT'S VITAMIN C! HAHAHAHA!

WHAT STAYS HOT EVEN IN THE FRIDGE? *MUSTARD!* ALSO, SPICY SALSA. HAHAHAHA!

What did one block of cheese say to the other? LET'S GROW MOULD TOGETHER!

MAN, EGGS ARE REALLY OVERRATED. YEAH, THEY'RE NOT ALL THEY'RE ***CRACKED UP*** TO BE!

I'D LOVE TO MAKE A JOKE ABOUT BUTTER, BUT I THINK THE ***MARGARINE*** FOR ERROR IS TOO GREAT.

HOW DO YOU MAKE A BUTTERFLY?
FLICK IT OUT OF THE DISH WITH A KNIFE! GET IT? HAHAHAHA!

SOMETHING FISHY

HEY, FISH! WHY DO YOU LIVE IN SALTWATER?
IS IT BECAUSE PEPPER MAKES YOU SNEEZE?

HEY, WHAT KIND OF FISH CAN'T SWIM? ***DEAD ONES!*** HAHAHAHAHA!

HEY YOU!

WAITER! BRING ME THE LOBSTER, AND MAKE IT

SNAPPY!

HAHAHA HA HAHA!

WHAT KIND OF FISH TASTES BETTER WITH ICE CREAM?
A JELLYFISH!

HEY! WHEN YOU'RE PREPARING FISH, IT'S REALLY EASY TO WEIGH THEM. DO YOU KNOW WHY? **BECAUSE THEY HAVE THEIR OWN SCALES!** HAHAHAHA!

WHAT KIND OF MUSIC DO FISH LIKE TO LISTEN TO? **SOMETHING CATCHY!** HAHAHAHA!

Meat and Greet

Ah, we **MEAT** again!

HEY! WHAT DO YOU CALL A COW WITH NO LEGS? *GROUND BEEF!* GET IT? HAHAHAHA!

HEY, ROAST BEEF! WHY ARE YOU SO TOUGH? IS IT BECAUSE YOU'RE FULL OF *IRON?*

WHERE DO HAMBURGERS BOX? *IN AN ONION RING!*

DO YOU KNOW WHAT YOU GET IF YOU CROSS A CHICKEN WITH A COW? *ROOST BEEF!*

HEY, HOT DOG! YOU LOOK LIKE YOU'VE GONE OFF! YEAH, ***YOU'RE A RANK-FURTER NOW!*** HAHAHAHA!

DO YOU KNOW HOW TO MAKE A CHICKEN STEW? ***KEEP IT WAITING FOR AGES!***

WHERE DO DEAD CHICKENS GO? ***TO OVEN!*** HAHAHAHA!

NYAH, NYAH, NYAH

WHAT DO YOU SAY TO CHICKENS BEFORE A PERFORMANCE? ***BREAK AN EGG!***

Where do tough chickens come from? HARD-BOILED EGGS.

GRRR

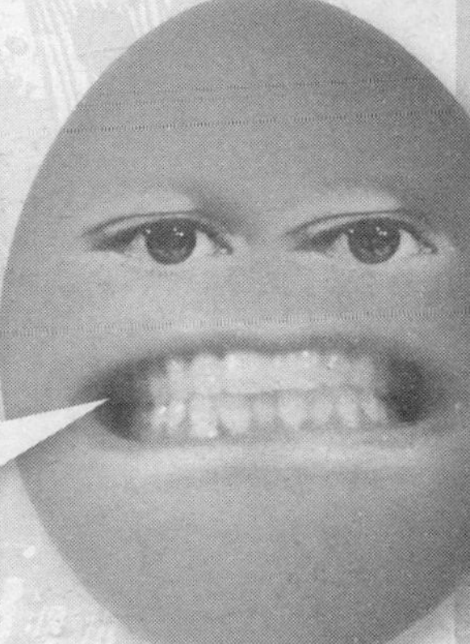

WHY ARE HAMBURGERS BETTER THAN HOT DOGS? ***BECAUSE HOT DOGS ARE THE WURST!*** HAHAHAHA!

WAZZUUUP!!

HEY! IF PIGS COULD FLY, ***WOULD THAT MEAN THE PRICE OF BACON WOULD GO UP?***

VEGETARIANS

So I was thinking about becoming a vegetarian, but then I realised it would be a MISSED STEAK. Hahahaha!

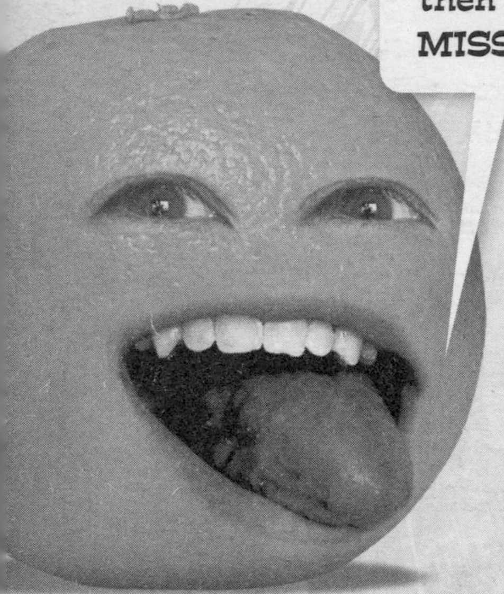

HEY! I SAW THIS GIRL EARLIER IN A VEGETARIAN RESTAURANT. ***SHE SAID SHE KNEW ME, BUT I'D NEVER MET HERBIVORE!*** HAHAHAHA!

HEY, HEY VEGETARIANS! IF YOU'RE TRYING TO SAVE THE ANIMALS, ***WHY ARE YOU EATING ALL THEIR FOOD?*** HAHAHAHA!

HEY! WHY DID THE TOFU CROSS THE ROAD? ***TO PROVE HE WASN'T CHICKEN!*** HAHAHAHAHA!

DO YOU KNOW WHAT A VEGETARIAN EARNS? DO YOU? DO YOU? ***A CELERY!*** GET IT?

My buddy had a carrot sticking out of one ear, celery out of the other and a spring onion up his nose. He went to the doctor to ask what was wrong. The doctor said, 'WELL, YOU'RE NOT EATING RIGHT.' Hahahahaha!
WHAT DID ONE VEGETARIAN SPY SAY TO THE OTHER?
WE HAVE TO STOP MEATING LIKE THIS!
HA HA HA HA HA
HEY! I FOLLOW A STRICT VEGETARIAN DIET. I ONLY EAT VEGETARIANS! HAHAHAHAHA!

BREAKING NEWS

Three cracked eggs found in fridge last night

Another one bites the CRUST – pizza restaurant closes down

Apple praised for his CORE VALUES

WORLD NEWS

LOL! LOL! LOL!

Girl found suffering from amnesia with sausages on her head – POLICE ARE CALLING HER BARBIE FOR NOW

Chopped Tomatoes CANNED from job at factory

HOW REFRESHING!

When I drink hot chocolate I get a pain in my eye. Weird, right?

Try taking the spoon out.

WHAT DO YOU CALL FIVE BOTTLES OF COLA?
A POP GROUP.

Hey, if you drank hot chocolate every day, would that make you a COCOA-NUT? Hahahaha!

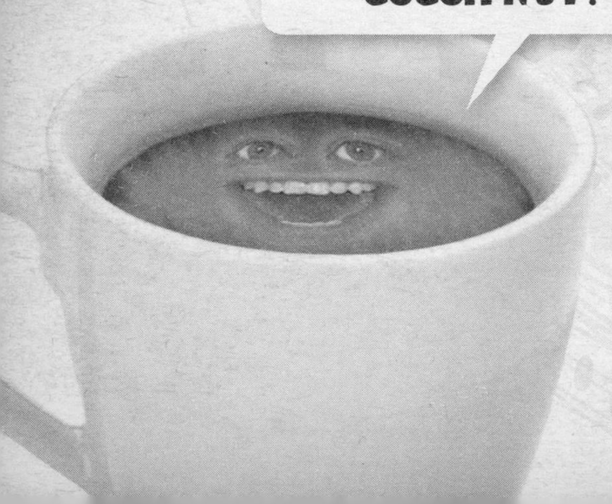

HEY, THIS COFFEE TASTES LIKE MUD! I GUESS IT'S ***BECAUSE IT WAS FRESHLY GROUND!*** GET IT?

HEY, HOT CHOCOLATE! YOU REALLY NEED TO LET OFF *SOME STEAM!* HAHAHAHA!

WHAT TEA DO SCIENTISTS DRINK?
GRAVI-TEA!

EGGS-ELLENT BREAKFAST

Ah, breakfast – the most important meal of the day. You know what they say – a boiled egg in the morning is HARD TO BEAT! Hahahaha!

Why did the bacon moan? BECAUSE THE EGGS' YOLKS WERE SO BAD.

HEY! DID YOU HEAR THE ONE ABOUT THE PORRIDGE? *YEAH, IT'S A LOAD OF MUSH!* HAHAHAHA!

HEY, WHICH TWO THINGS CAN'T YOU HAVE FOR BREAKFAST? *LUNCH AND DINNER!* HAHAHAHA!

HEY, HEY YOU! DO YOU KNOW WHAT CATS EAT FOR BREAKFAST? *MICE CRISPIES!* HAHAHAHAHA!

HEY! HEY! HEY!

HEY, IF YOU'RE FRENCH, WHAT DO YOU EAT AT EIGHT O'CLOCK IN THE MORNING? *HUIT-HEURE-BIX.* HAHAHAHAHA!

AND WHY DON'T THE FRENCH HAVE TWO EGGS FOR BREAKFAST? *BECAUSE ONE EGG IS UN OEUF!* HAHAHAHA!

Why is a pancake like a cricket team? **BECAUSE THEY BOTH NEED A GOOD BATTER!** Hahahaha!

Hey, Pancake! Where do you live? **DO YOU LIVE IN A FLAT?** Hahahaha!

TIME FOR LUNCH

What's the best way to stop your lunch going off?
EAT IT!

HEY, SANDWICH! DID YOU KNOW IT'S IMPOSSIBLE TO STARVE IN THE DESERT? ***YEAH, BECAUSE OF ALL THE SAND-WHICH-IS THERE!*** HAHAHAHA!

WHAT LOOKS LIKE HALF A SANDWICH? ***THE OTHER HALF!***

KNIFE!!!...

HOW CAN YOU MAKE YOUR SOUP RICH?
ADD FOURTEEN CARROTS.

HEY, CREAM OF TOMATO! YOU'RE A COMPLETE IDIOT.
YEAH, *YOU'RE A REAL NINCOM-SOUP.* GET IT?

HEY, WHAT DID THE WAITRESS SAY WHEN THE CUSTOMER
KNOCKED THEIR SOUP ALL OVER HER? SHE SAID
'LUNCH IS ON ME!'

What did one tortilla
chip say to the other?

LET'S GO
FOR A DIP!

WHAT'S FOR DINNER?

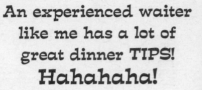

An experienced waiter like me has a lot of great dinner TIPS! Hahahaha!

CUSTOMER: WAITER, I DON'T LIKE CHEESE WITH HOLES IN IT.
WAITER: WELL, JUST EAT THE CHEESE AND LEAVE THE HOLES.

CUSTOMER: WAITER, I'D LIKE TO KNOW WHAT'S IN TONIGHT'S STEW.
WAITER: NO, SIR, YOU WOULDN'T.

CUSTOMER: WAITER, WHY IS MY PIE ALL SQUASHED?
WAITER: YOU DID ASK ME TO STEP ON IT, SIR.

CUSTOMER: WAITER, IS THIS ALL YOU HAVE FOR DINNER?
WAITER: NO SIR, I'LL BE HAVING A LOVELY ROAST WHEN I GET HOME.

Waiter, there's a fly in my soup!

DON'T WORRY, THE SPIDER ON THE ROLL WILL CATCH IT.

CUSTOMER: WAITER, I SIMPLY CAN'T EAT THIS DISGUSTING FOOD. FETCH ME THE MANAGER!
WAITER: THAT WON'T HELP, MADAM. HE WON'T EAT IT EITHER.

CUSTOMER: WAITER, WHAT IS THIS?
WAITER: IT'S A STRAWBERRY SURPRISE.
CUSTOMER: BUT I CAN'T SEE ANY STRAWBERRIES!
WAITER: THAT'S THE SURPRISE.

WHAT DID ONE PLATE OF LEFTOVERS SAY TO THE OTHER?
FOILED AGAIN!
HAHAHAHA!

HEY YOU!

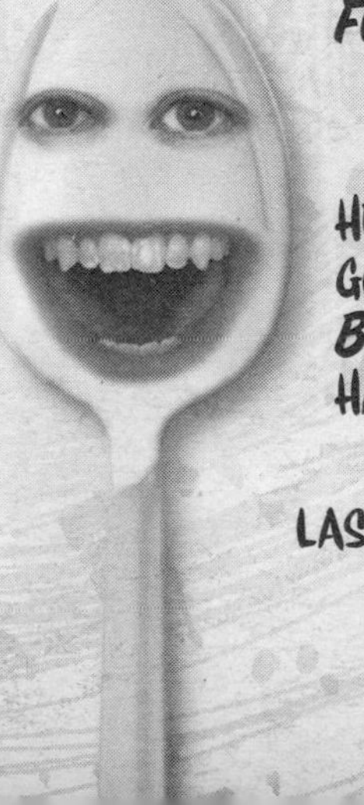

HEY, WHY ARE WAITERS GOOD AT MULTIPLICATION?
BECAUSE THEY KNOW THEIR TABLES!
HAHAHAHA!

LAST NIGHT I LEFT DINNER AFTER THE MAIN COURSE. ***I GUESS THAT MAKES ME A DESSERTER!***

JUST DESSERTS

My pudding jokes are FLANTASTIC! Hahahaha!

Hey, Ice Cream! DID YOU GO TO SUNDAE SCHOOL? Hahahahaha!

HEY! HOW DO YOU START A PUDDING RACE? *SAGO!*

AND HOW DO YOU START A JELLY RACE? *GET SET!* HAHAHAHAHA!

AND WHAT'S THE FASTEST CAKE IN THE WORLD? *SCONE!*

WHAT'S YELLOW AND STUPID? *THICK CUSTARD!*

WHAT'S THE HARDEST CAKE IN THE WORLD?
MARBLE CAKE!

WHAT KIND OF CAKE CAN YOU EAT IN THE BATH?
A SPONGE CAKE!

WHAT DO YOU CALL A JELLY ON A PLANE?
A JET SETTER! GET IT? WHY AREN'T YOU LAUGHING?

HOW DO YOU MAKE FAIRY CAKES?
WITH ELF-RAISING FLOUR.

WHY DID THE JELLY WOBBLE?
BECAUSE IT SAW THE MILK SHAKE! HAHAHAHA!

HEY! DO YOU KNOW WHAT SITS IN CUSTARD, LOOKING CROSS?
IT'S APPLE GRUMBLE!

SWEET TREATS

These are for you, Marshmallow!

yaaaaay! Sweet jokes! I love sweet jokes!

WHAT KIND OF SWEET GOES SWINGING THROUGH THE JUNGLE? *TARZIPAN!*

WHAT KIND OF SWEETS DO FROGS LIKE? *LOLLI-HOPS!*

DO YOU KNOW WHAT KIND OF BISCUIT CAN FLY? *A PLANE ONE!*

GET IT? GET IT?

HEY, FLYING SAUCER! *YOU'RE SUCH AN AIRHEAD!*

NYAH, NYAH, NYAH

HEY, IF YOU EAT TOO MUCH *FUDGE*, WILL YOU HAVE SO MUCH *PUDGE* THAT YOU WON'T BE ABLE TO *BUDGE?* HAHAHAHA

GINGERBREAD MEN ARE A REALLY GREAT SNACK IF YOU'RE FEELING CROSS. KNOW WHY? *'COZ EACH ONE GIVES YOU THE CHANCE TO BITE SOMEONE'S HEAD OFF!*

AAAAH!!

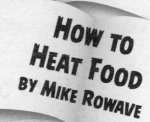

WAZZUUUP!

PERFECT PANCAKES
BY MABEL SYRUP

TEATIME SNACKS
BY DUNCAN A. BISCUIT

HOW TO COOK PASTA
BY AL DENTE

GROW YOUR OWN VEGETABLES
BY ARTY CHOKE

THE BASICS OF LUNCH
BY ROLAND BUTTER

THE MOST AWESOME JOKE BOOK IN THE WORLD BY JOE KING

TOOLS OF THE TRADE

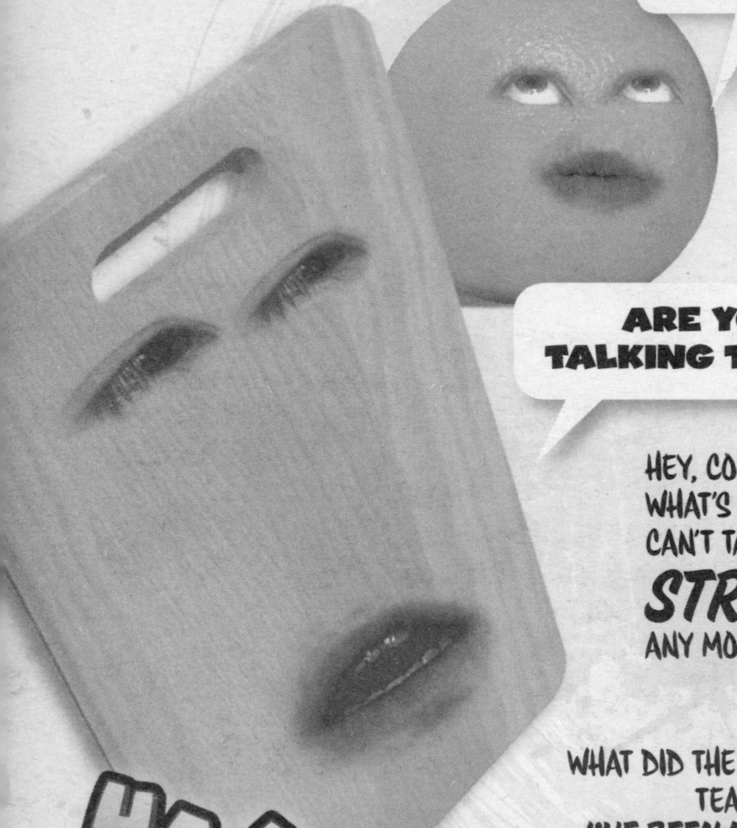

HEY, COLANDER! WHAT'S UP? CAN'T TAKE THE ***STRAIN*** ANY MORE?

WHAT DID THE CRACKED TEACUP SAY? ***I'VE BEEN MUGGED!***

What did the plate say
to the cup?
DINNER IS ON ME.
Hahahaha!

HEY, WHAT KIND OF
DANCE DOES A TIN
OPENER DO?
THE CAN CAN!
GET IT?
HAHAHAHA!

WHAT DID THE TIN SAY TO THE
TIN OPENER?
YOU MAKE ME FLIP MY LID!

AND WHAT GETS WETTER
THE MORE IT DRIES?
A TEA TOWEL!

WHAT DID THE PEELER SAY TO THE CARROT?
'YOU THOUGHT I WAS THE WORST THING THAT WOULD
HAPPEN TO YOU TODAY, BUT THERE'S *GRATER* DANGER
JUST AROUND THE CORNER!'

WHAT CAN YOU PUT IN A CUP
BUT NOT TAKE OUT AGAIN?
A CRACK!

HEY!

DO YOU WANT
TO HEAR THE
JOKE ABOUT THE
KITCHEN BIN?
NAH, IT'S
RUBBISH!

CLOSE ENCOUNTERS OF THE ANNOYING KIND

Man, everything's been a bit weird around here recently. We've had several close encounters of the annoying kind with some alien beings. But at least it's given me the opportunity to work on my space jokes! **Yeah!**

Aah, the specimens are conscious! Let's take them by surprise while the orange one tries to be funny.

HEY, DO YOU KNOW WHY ALIENS ALWAYS SPILL THEIR TEA? *BECAUSE OF THEIR FLYING SAUCERS!*

DO YOU KNOW WHAT KIND OF SWEETS ALIENS EAT? *MARTIAN-MALLOWS!* HAHAHAHA!

WHAT DID THE HUNGRY ALIEN
SAY WHEN HE CAME TO EARTH?

Take me to your larder!

Hey, what do you get if
you cross a UFO with a
rasher of bacon?
A FRYING SAUCER!

AND WHAT KIND OF NUTS
CAN YOU FIND IN SPACE?
ASTRO-NUTS!

HEY, MOON! I CAN TELL
YOU'VE HAD ENOUGH TO
EAT. *YEAH, BECAUSE
YOU'RE A FULL MOON.*
GET IT? FULL?

WHAT DO YOU CALL AN
ALIEN WITH THREE EYES?
AN ALIIIEN!
HAHAHAHAHA!

OUT AND ABOUT

Why couldn't any customers get into the fish and chip shop? BECAUSE THE FISH FILLET!

Hey, Baker! Do you share your recipes on a KNEAD TO KNOW BASIS? Hahahaha!

Hey, Chef! How do you keep track of your earnings? DO YOU USE A PIE CHART? Hahahaha!

Hey, Baker! WHAT'S YOUR FLOURLY RATE? Hahahaha!

HEY, WHAT'S THE BEST WAY TO KEEP YOUR FOOD BILLS DOWN? USE A PAPERWEIGHT!

HA HA HA HA HA!

How do you make a hot dog stand? TAKE AWAY ITS CHAIR!

HEY!

CHRISTMAS CRACKERS

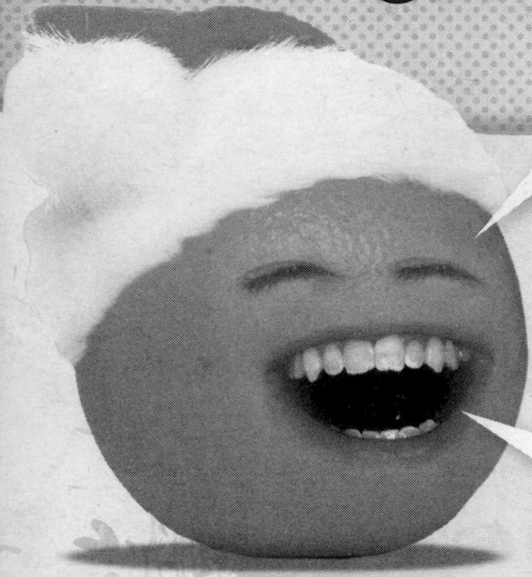

NYAH, NYAH, NYAH

HEY! DO YOU KNOW WHO'S NEVER HUNGRY AT CHRISTMAS? *TURKEY, BECAUSE HE'S ALWAYS STUFFED!*

WHAT'S BROWN AND SNEAKS AROUND THE KITCHEN?

MINCE SPIES!

HOW DOES GOOD KING WENCESLAS LIKE HIS PIZZA?
DEEP PAN, CRISP AND EVEN!

HEY! IF YOUR CHRISTMAS DINNER GETS BURNED,
SHOULD YOU SAY *'MERRY CRISPNESS'*?
HAHAHAHA!

What's the best thing to put in a Christmas pudding? YOUR TEETH! Hahahaha!

SILLY SIGNS

OMG! It's not just me! Check out these awesome shop signs! Hahahahaha!

RELISH THE THOUGHT
THE FINEST BURGERS IN TOWN

A BREWED AWAKENING
SERVING COFFEE ALL DAY

LETTUCE EAT
FINE SALADS SINCE 2008

MEN AT WOK
DELICIOUS CHINESE FOOD

FAST FOOD FUNNIES

Read them quick or you might miss them! Hahahaha!

WHY DID THE MAN CLIMB UP ONTO THE ROOF OF THE FAST FOOD RESTAURANT? *BECAUSE THEY TOLD HIM HIS MEAL WAS ON THE HOUSE!*

HEY! HEY! YOU!

HEY, HOT DOG! I HEAR YOU CAN'T STOP MAKING JOKES. *I GUESS IT'S BECAUSE YOU'RE ON A ROLL!*

HEY! IF YOU STEAL SOMEONE ELSE'S TAKE-AWAY CURRY, DO YOU GET ***BAD KORMA?*** HAHAHAHA!

Do you know where burgers like to dance? AT A MEATBALL! Hahahaha!

Hey, how do we know burgers like young people? Because they're PRO-TEEN! Hahahaha!

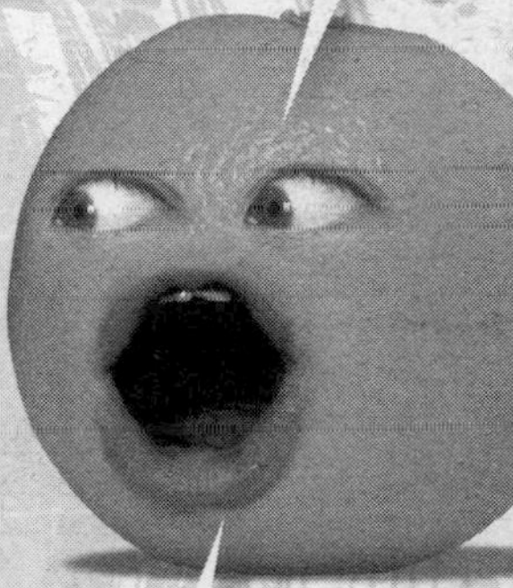

Hey, Hamburger! Hey! Could you marry a hot dog? I guess you could, if you had a very FRANK RELATIONSHIP! Get it? Hahahaha!

WHAT KIND OF MONSTER LOVES FAST FOOD?

ZOOM-BIE FRUIT!

GRUESOME GIGGLES

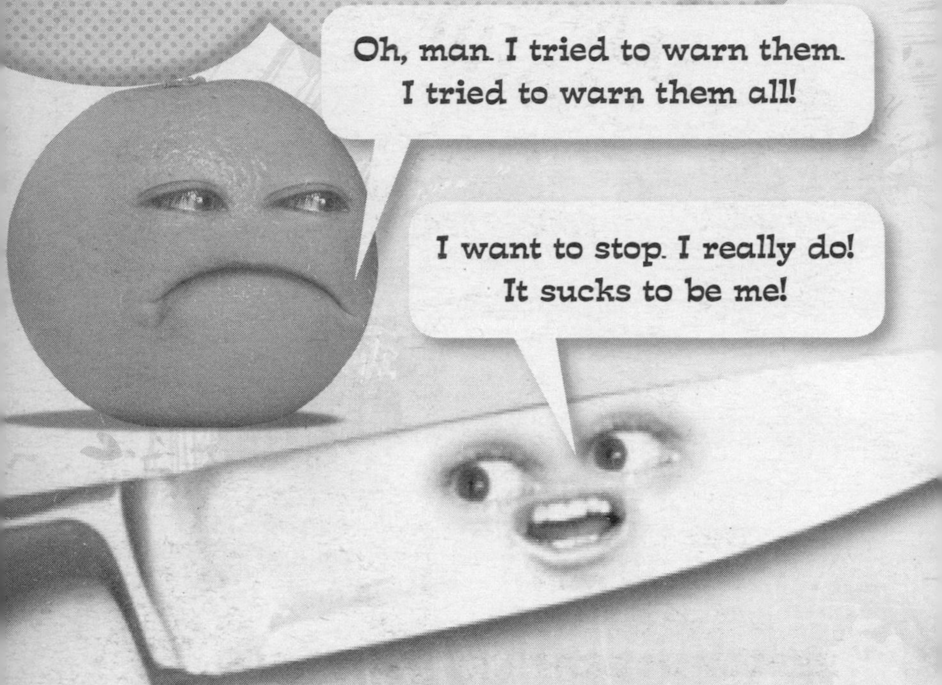

HEY! DO YOU KNOW HOW MANY KNIVES IT TAKES TO CHANGE A LIGHTBULB? OR WOULD IT JUST BE A STAB IN THE DARK? HAHAHAHA!

HEY! BREAD ROLL! I BET YOU NEVER SAW BREAD KNIFE COMING! GET IT? SAW? HAHAHAHA!

KNIFE

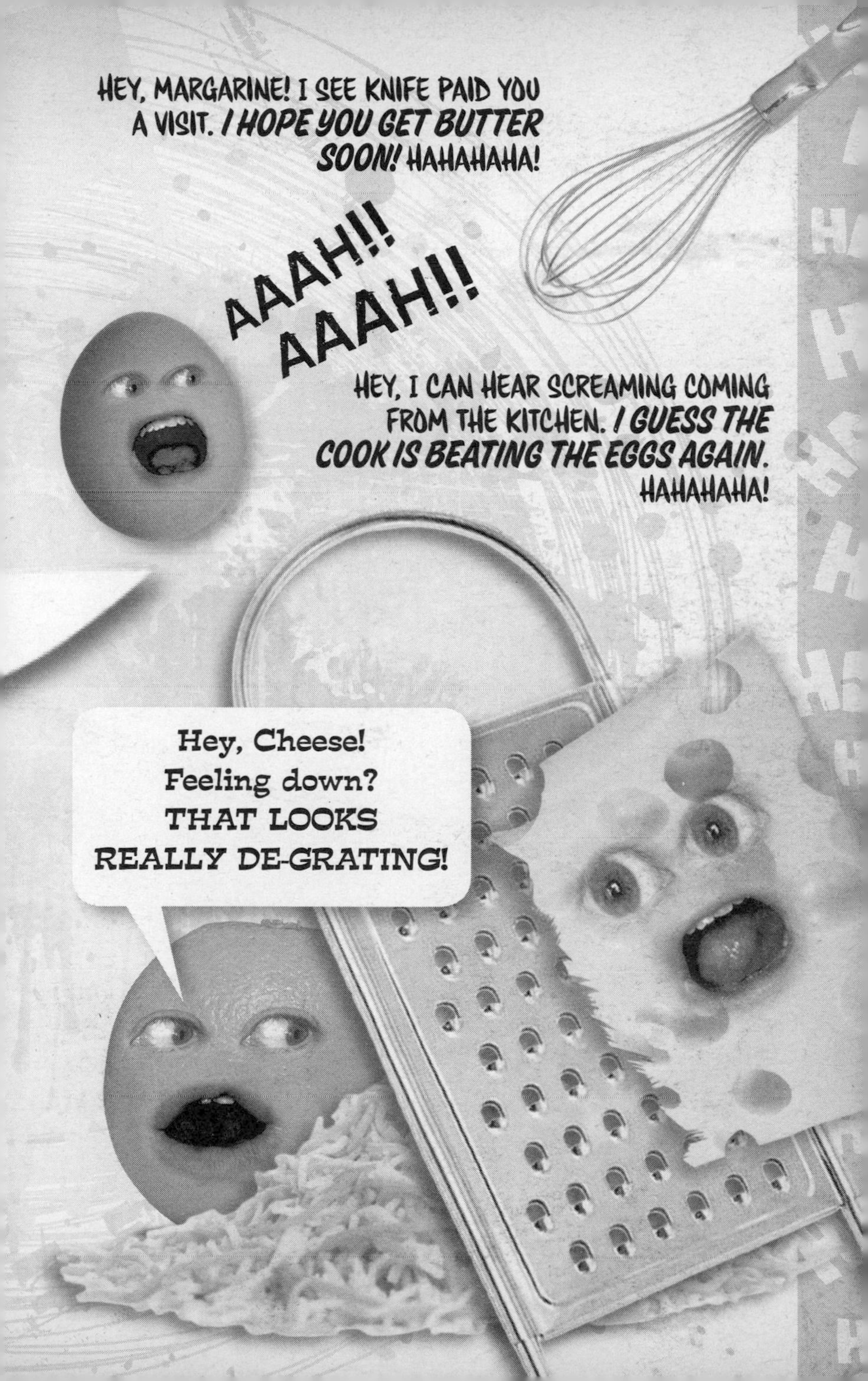
HEY, MARGARINE! I SEE KNIFE PAID YOU A VISIT. *I HOPE YOU GET BUTTER SOON!* HAHAHAHA!
AAAH!! AAAH!!
HEY, I CAN HEAR SCREAMING COMING FROM THE KITCHEN. *I GUESS THE COOK IS BEATING THE EGGS AGAIN.* HAHAHAHA!
Hey, Cheese! Feeling down? THAT LOOKS REALLY DE-GRATING!

WORLD FOOD

WHAT'S 200 FEET TALL, MADE OF SPONGE AND JELLY AND FOUND IN THE CENTRE OF PARIS?
THE TRIFLE TOWER!

WHERE DO THEY SERVE THE COLDEST FOOD?
IN CHILE!
HAHAHAHA!

WHY DO THE FRENCH EAT SNAILS? ***IS IT BECAUSE THEY DON'T LIKE FAST FOOD?*** HAHAHAHAHA!

WHICH COUNTRY SATISFIES HUNGARY?
TURKEY!
WHERE DO DISHES COME FROM?
CHINA!
HEY, IRISH POTATO! DID YOU KNOW YOU CAN CHANGE YOUR NATIONALITY?
YEAH – BY BECOMING A FRENCH FRY!
HAHAHAHA!
Hey, Mexican Food! What's up?
DON'T YOU WANNA TACO BOUT IT?
It's nacho problem, amigo.

YOU NEED HELP!

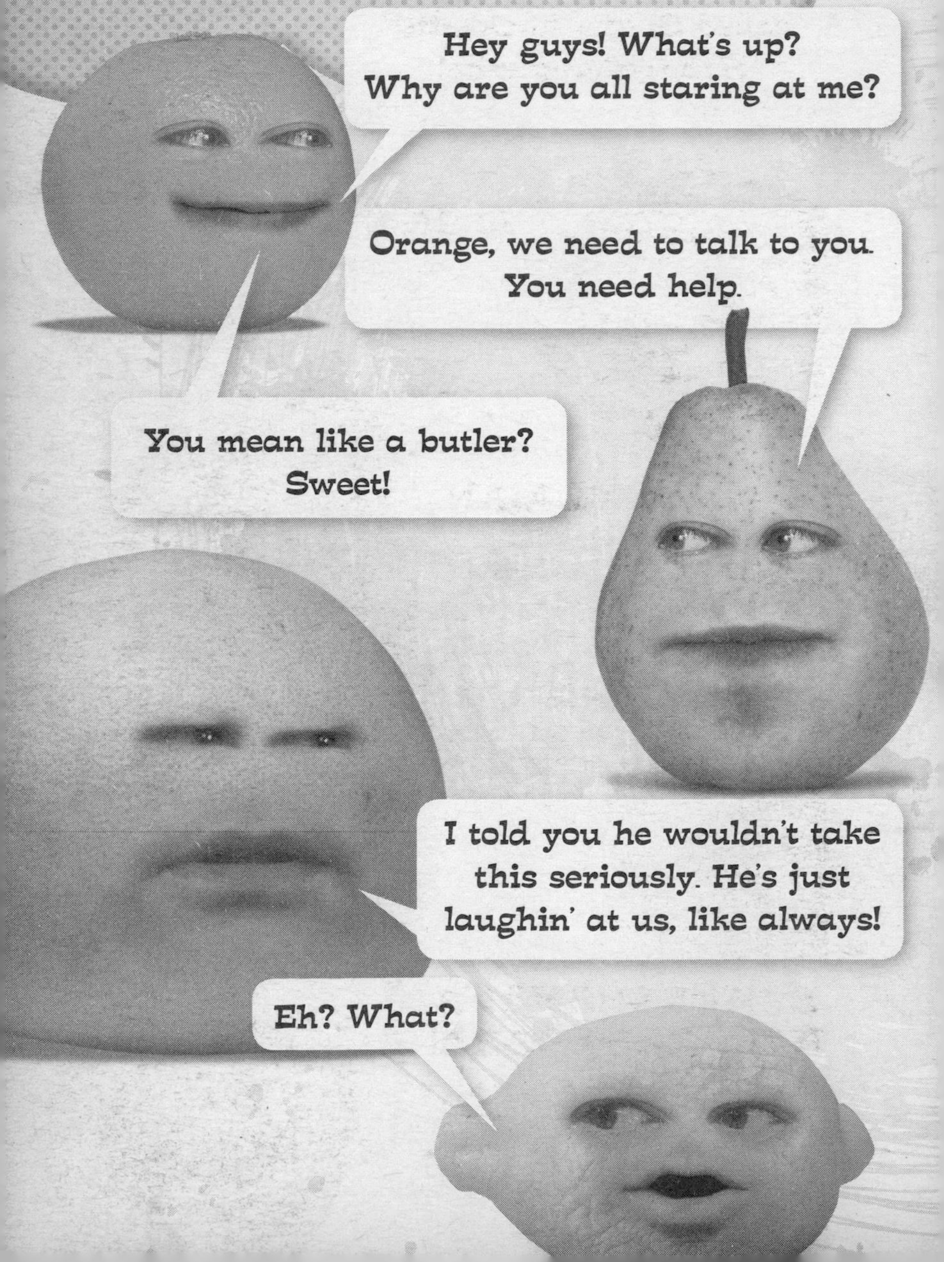

For your information, I have a condition that makes me laugh uncontrollably. It's called Gigglechuckleitis! Hahahahahahaha!
SERIOUSLY?
OH, MAN...
I give up.
HAHAHAHAHAHA HAHAHAHAHAHA!